2 Workbook

Pippa and Pop

American English

Colin Sage

with Caroline Nixon & Michael Tomlinson

CAMBRIDGE
UNIVERSITY PRESS

Map of the book

	VOCABULARY	LANGUAGE	SOUNDS AND LETTERS	LITERACY AND VALUES	NUMBERS	CROSS-CURRICULAR
Introduction Page 4						
1 Hello! Page 6	Review Level 1: characters, clothes, colors, nature, objects, school, toys *black, gray, orange, purple, white*	Review Level 1: *I'm (Kim).* *I'm a (girl).* *I like (books).* *Draw (a butterfly).* *Color / Paint it (purple).*	Review Level 1 letter sounds: *a, e, i, o, u*	*The colorful chameleon* Celebrate differences	Review numbers: *1 – 10*	Art: Mixing colors
2 My family Page 18	*aunt, uncle, cousin, grandma, grandpa* *funny, old, short, tall, young*	*Who's that?* *He's my (grandpa).* *She's my (grandma).* *She's / He's / I'm (old).* *She isn't / He isn't / I'm not (young).*	Letter sounds: *d, m*	*Anna's baby brother* Be patient	Numbers: *11, 12*	Science: Growing up
3 My home Page 30	*bathroom, bedroom, dining room, kitchen, living room* *cooking, eating, playing, sleeping, washing*	*Where's (Kim / Dan / Dan's mommy)?* *She's / He's in the (kitchen).* *What's she / he doing?* *She's / He's (sleeping).*	Letter sounds: *b, k*	*Hide-and-seek* Be careful	Numbers: *13, 14*	Math: Shapes
Units 1–3 Review Page 42						
4 My body Page 44	*fingers, head, neck, shoulders, toes* *blond, curly, long, short, straight (hair)*	*She / He / It has (a neck).* *She / He / It has (long) hair.* *She / He / It doesn't have (short) hair.*	Letter sounds: *t, n*	*Milo's shadow* Be resilient	One less	Science: Shadows
5 Outdoors Page 56	*cold, hot, rainy, sunny, windy* *boots, raincoat, sandals, sunglasses, sweater*	*What's the weather like?* *It's (hot).* *I'm wearing (a raincoat).*	Letter sounds: *s, h*	*Rainy day fun* Celebrate nature	Numbers: *15, 16*	Science: Rainbows

	VOCABULARY	LANGUAGE	SOUNDS AND LETTERS	LITERACY AND VALUES	NUMBERS	CROSS-CURRICULAR
⑥ Animals Page 68	chicken, cow, goat, horse, sheep fly, jump, run, swim, walk	It's a (horse). It has a (long) (neck). A (horse) can / can't (jump).	Letter sounds: c, g	Stubborn goats! Be considerate	More or less?	Social studies: How animals help us
Units 4–6 Review Page 80						
⑦ My favorite food Page 82	hamburger, lollipop, mango, orange, pear bread, cheese, eggs, fish, fries	Can I have (a pear), please? Do you like (fish)? Yes, I do. / No, I don't.	Letter sounds: f, l, p	Pea soup Be helpful	Numbers: 17, 18	Science: Where food comes from
⑧ My senses Page 94	feel, hear, see, smell, taste bee, grass, leaf, lemon, watermelon	Can you (see) (the rain)? Yes, I can. / No, I can't. What can you (hear)? I can (hear) a (bee).	Letter sounds: j, z	A wonderful day Enjoy the world around you	Recognizing patterns	Science: Loud and quiet
⑨ Vacations! Page 106	beach, ocean; boats, kites, shells drinking lemonade, eating ice cream, making sandcastles, playing with shells, taking pictures	How many (boats) can you see? I can see (four) (boats). I'm (playing with shells).	Letter sounds: v, w, y	You can do it, Sam! Persevere	Numbers: 19, 20	Science: Floating and sinking
Units 7–9 Review Page 118						

Welcome back!

👁 **Look.** 🔍 **Find.** ◯ **Circle.**

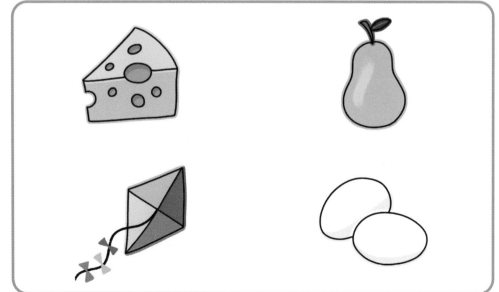

 Look. Match. Say.

1 Hello!

1 Unit topic introduction: Song practice

🎧 Listen again. 📖 Match. 💬 Say.

Language review: *Hello. I'm (Kim). I'm a (girl). I like (cars). I have a (yellow) (car).* 1

7

👁 Look. 🔍 Find. ⃝ Circle. 💬 Say.

1 Language practice: *Hello. I'm (Sue). I'm a (woman). I like (butterflies).*

🏠 **At home** Imagine your toy can talk. What does it say?

🎧 **⁶ Listen again.** 👁 **Look.** ◯ **Circle.** 💬 **Say.**

👁 Look. ☝ Point. ✏ Color.

👁 Look. 🔍 Find. ✏ Draw.

🏠 At home

How are you and your friends different?

👁 Look. ✏ Color. 💬 Say.

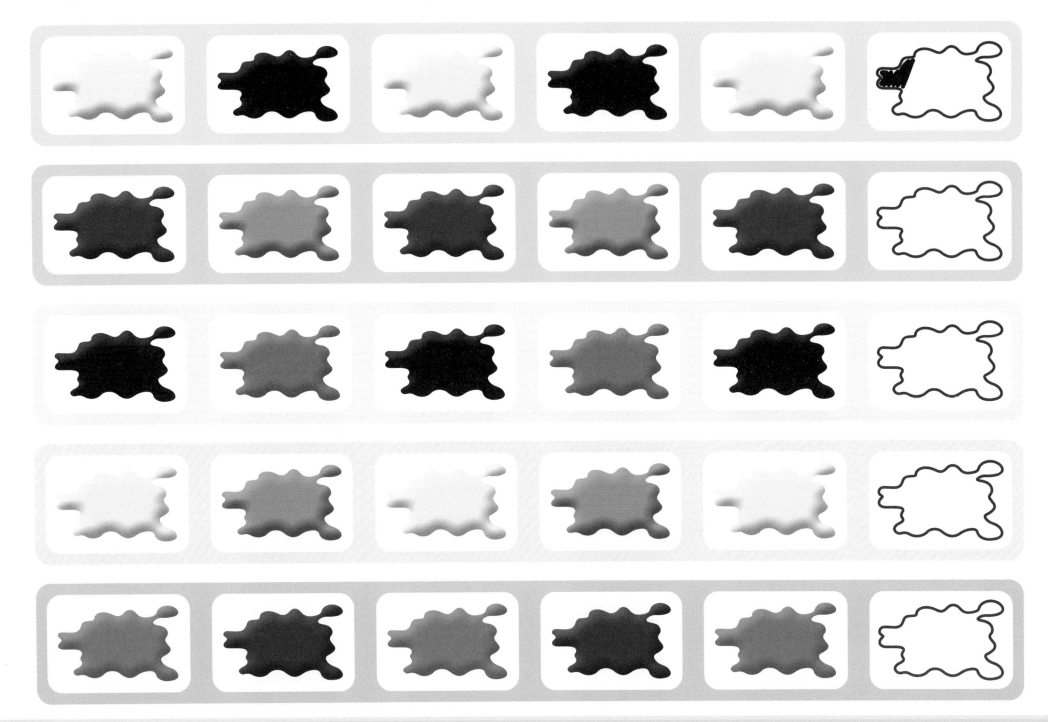

① Vocabulary practice: *white, black, purple, orange, gray*

⊙ Look. 🔍 Find. ◯ Circle. 💬 Say.

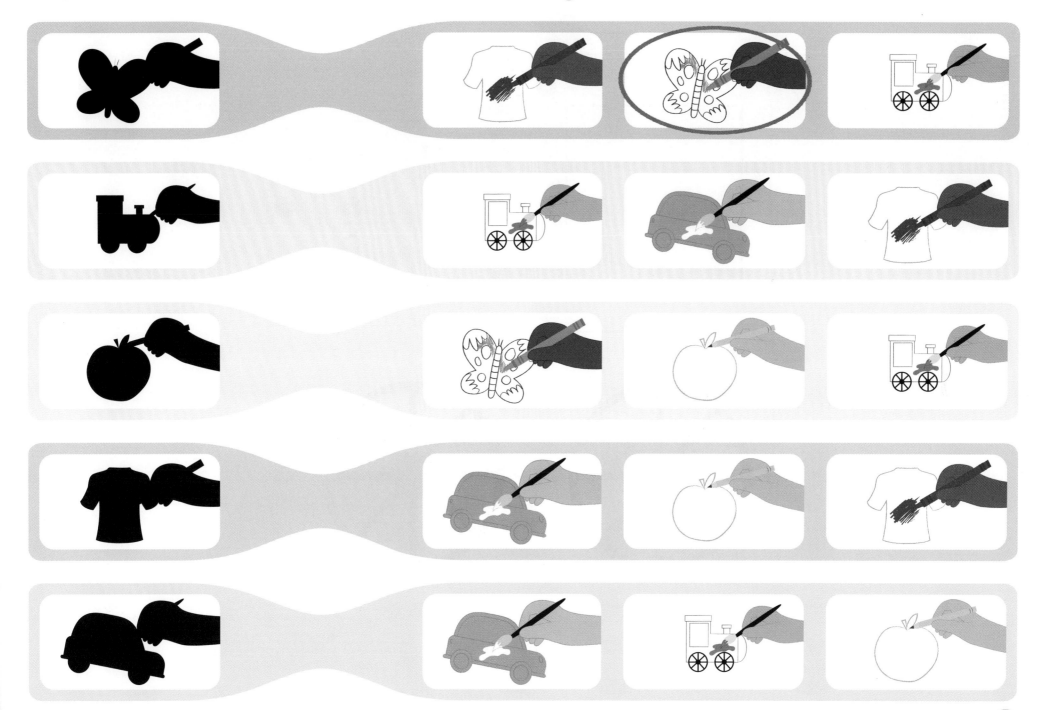

Look. ✏️ **Draw.** ✋ **Count.** 💬 **Say.**

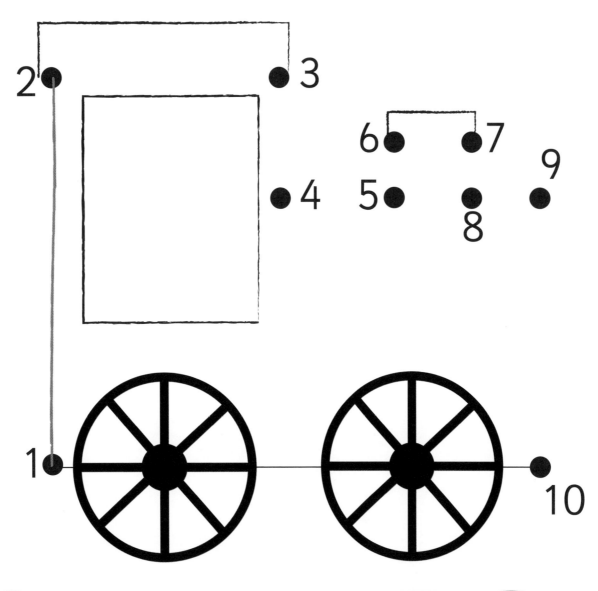

1 2 3 4 5 6 7 8 9 10

 **At home** Look in your house.
Find the numbers 1 to 10.

👁 **Look.** ✏ **Color.** 💬 **Say.**

👁 **Look.** ✏ **Draw.** 💬 **Say.**

I'm Dan. I'm a boy.
I like flowers.

1 *Hello. I'm (Dan). I'm a (boy). I like (flowers). I have a (yellow) (flower).*

Point. 💬 **Say.** ✏️ **Color.**

Draw a train.

Good job!

② My family

🎧 12 **Listen again.** 👁 **Look.** 🔘 **Stick.** 👆 **Point.**

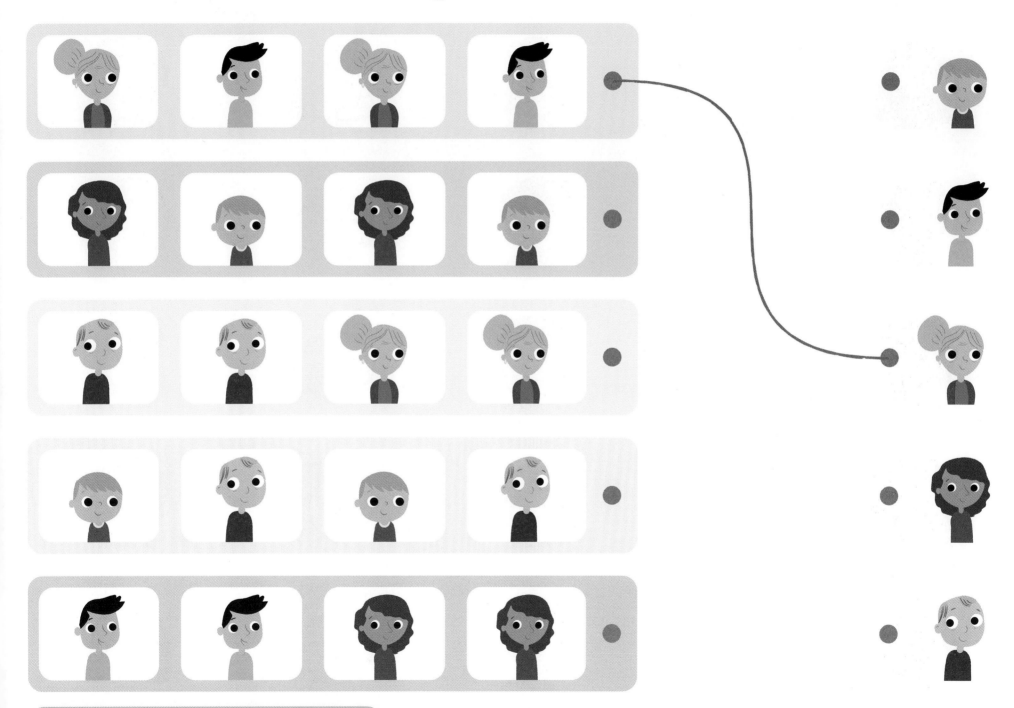 Look. Match. Say.

At home — Who's in your family? Say.

2   19

Vocabulary practice: *grandma, grandpa, aunt, uncle, cousin*

◉ Look. 🔍 Find. ◯ Circle. 💬 Say.

② Language practice: *Who's that? She's (Dan's / my) (grandma / aunt / cousin). He's (Dan's / my) (grandpa / uncle / cousin).*

15 🎧 **Listen again.** ✏️ **Color.** 💬 **Say.**

d m a m e d

d m

m u d a d m

2 Literacy practice: Anna's baby brother

👁 Look. ⭕ Trace.

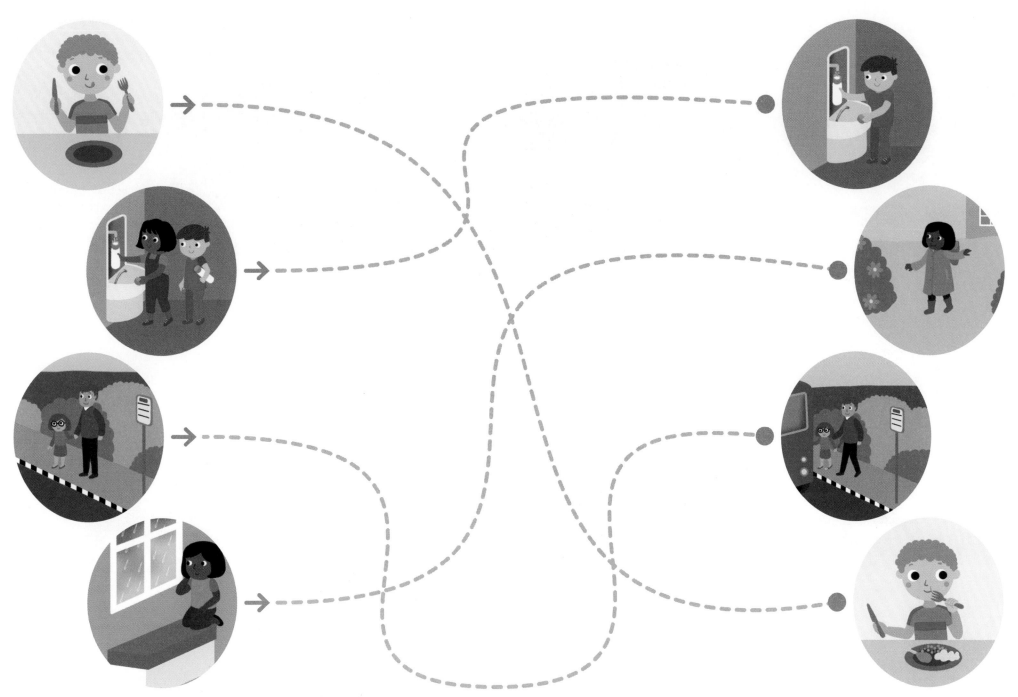

Look. Match. Say.

2 **Vocabulary practice:** *funny, young, tall, short, old*

◉ Look. 🔍 Find. ◯ Circle. 💬 Say.

👁 **Look.** ✋ **Count.** ◯ **Circle.** 💬 **Say.**

|  | 11 | 12 |

👁 Look. ✏ Color. 💬 Say.

At home Look at old pictures. Can you see your family growing up?

👁 **Look.** ✏ **Draw.** 💬 **Say.**

She's my grandma.

2 *Who's that? She's my (grandma / aunt / cousin). He's my (grandpa / uncle / cousin).*

 **Point.** 💬 **Say.** ✏️ **Color.**

She's tall.

Good job!

I'm / He's / She's (tall / young / funny / short / old). I'm not / He isn't / She isn't (tall).

③ My home

👁 Look. 📖 Match. 💬 Say.

🏠 **At home** Go to the rooms in your house. Say.

Vocabulary practice: *living room, bedroom, bathroom, kitchen, dining room* ③ 31

👁 Look. 🔍 Find. ⭕ Circle. 💬 Say.

3 **Language practice:** *Where's (Uncle / Aunt)? He's / She's in the (bathroom / bedroom / kitchen / dining room / living room).*

24 🎧 **Listen again.** ✏️ **Color.** 💬 **Say.**

👁 Look. 🔍 Find. ✏ Color.

🏠 At home

When are you careful?

👁 Look. 🔍 Find. ⭕ Circle. 💬 Say.

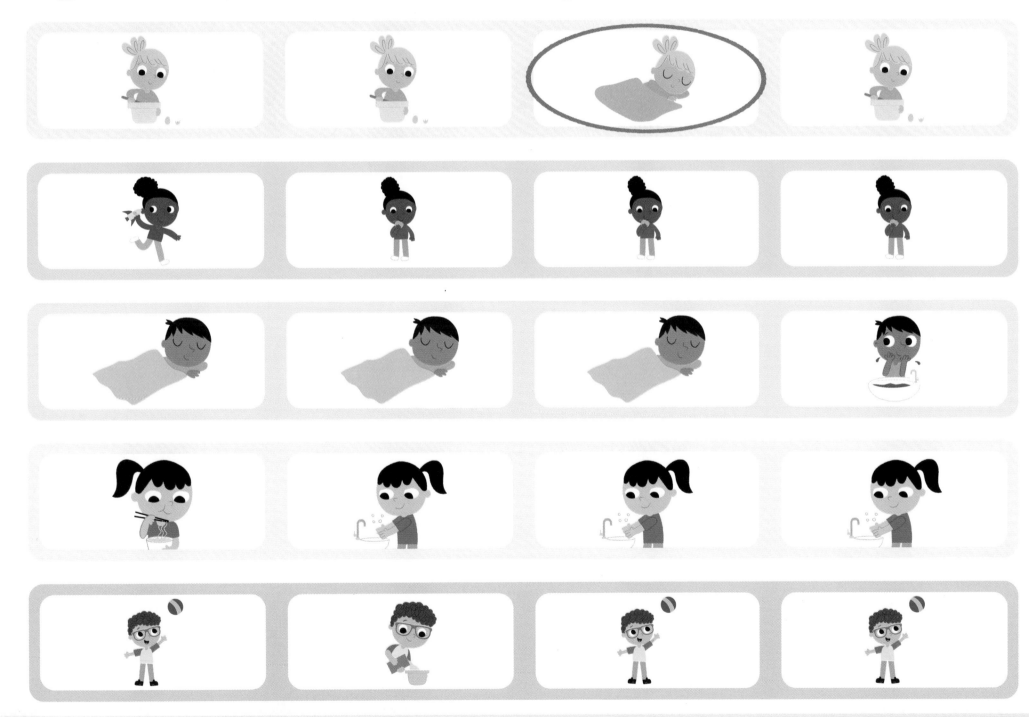

3 *Vocabulary practice: cooking, sleeping, playing, eating, washing*

Look. Match. Say.

👁 **Look.** ✋ **Count.** ◯ **Circle.** 💬 **Say.**

🚗	**13**	**14**

◯	**13**	**14**

👁 Look. 🔍 Find. ⭕ Trace. 💬 Say.

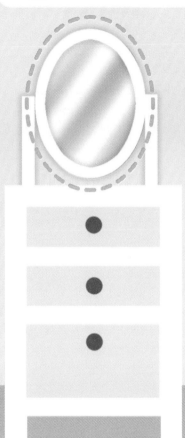
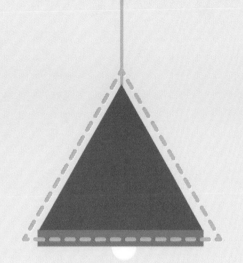

🏠 **At home**

Find an oval, a rectangle, a triangle, a circle, and a square. Say.

Look. Draw. Say.

He's eating.

3 *What's he / she doing? He's / She's (eating). He's / She's in the (living room).*

Point. 💬 **Say.** ✏️ **Color.**

He's in the bedroom.
He's sleeping.

Good job!

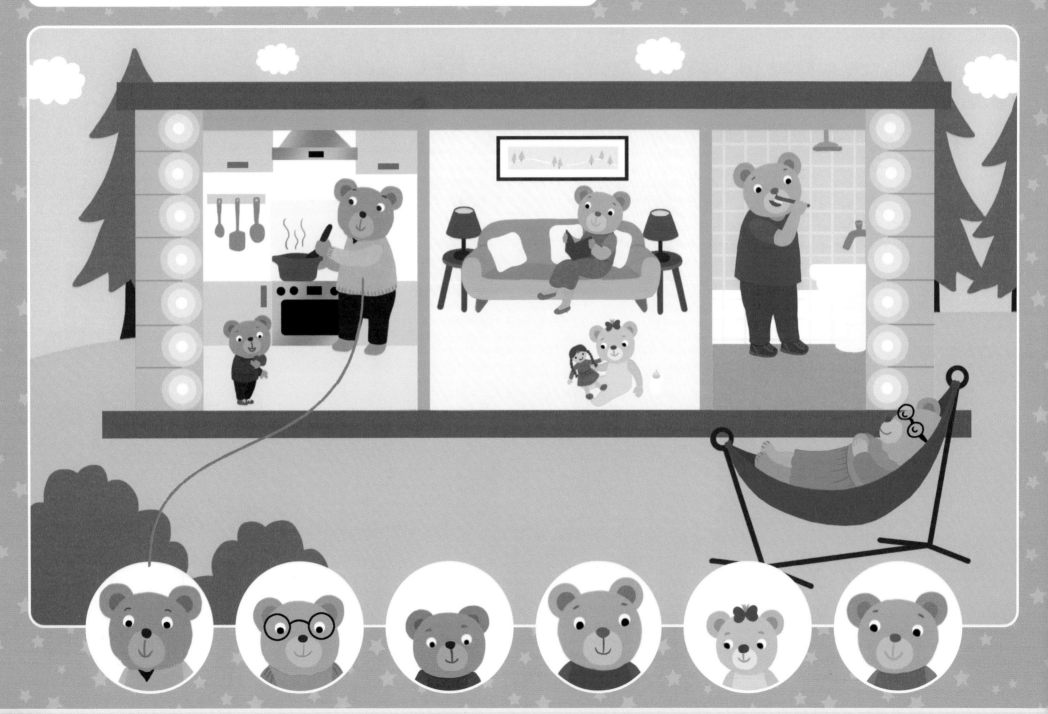

Look. Find. Match. Say.

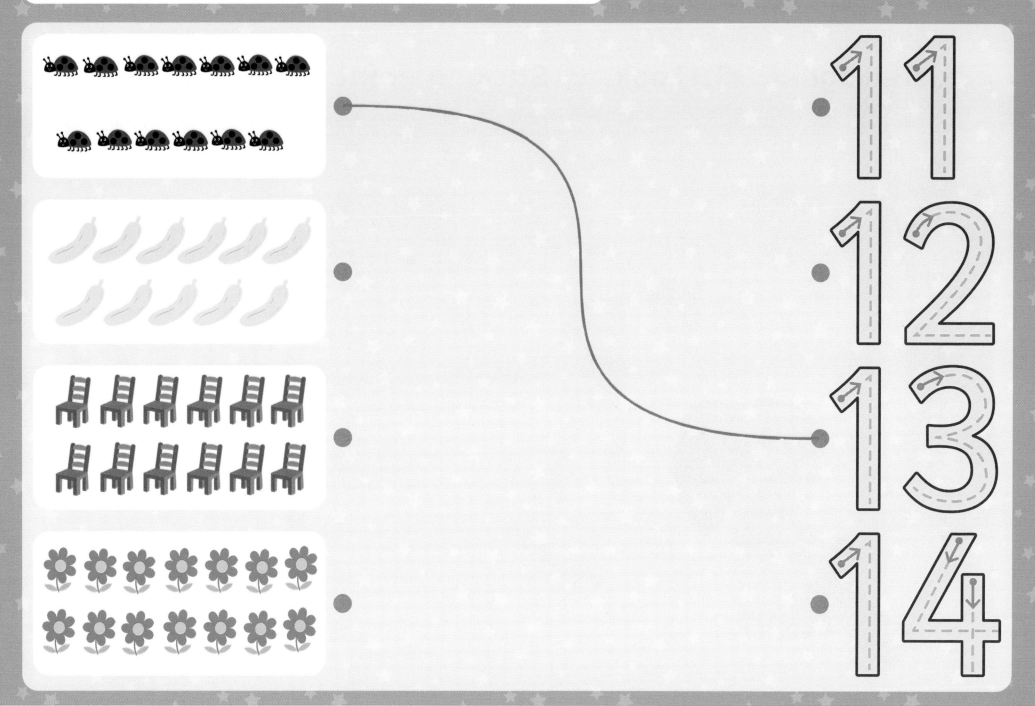

4 My body

👁 Look. 🔍 Find. ⭕ Circle. 💬 Say.

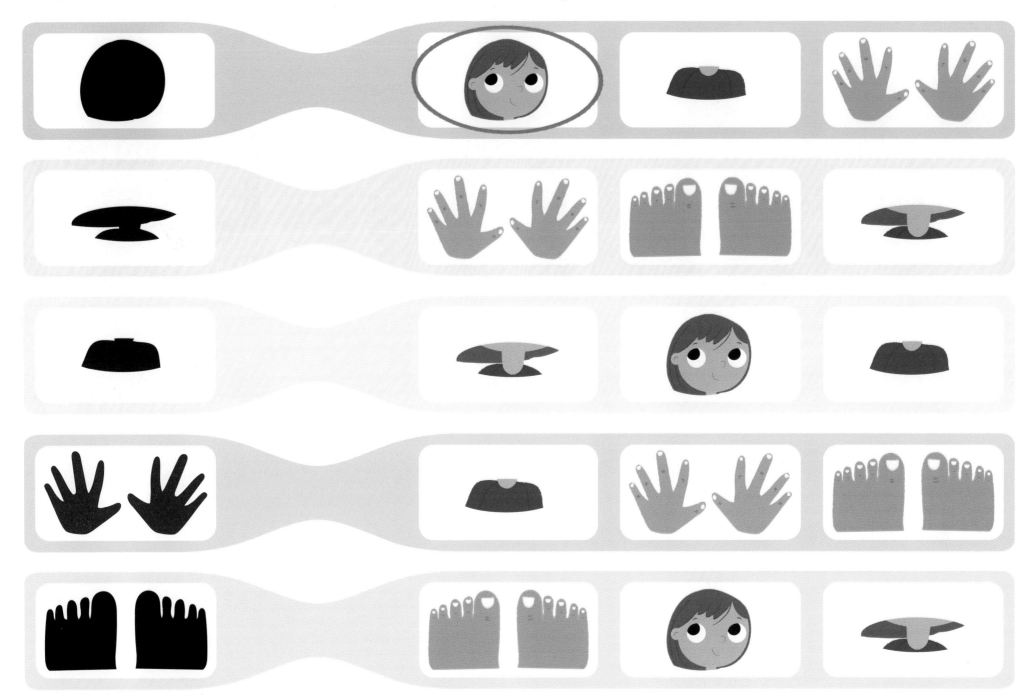

 **At home**   Find a doll. Point to the head, neck, shoulders, fingers, and toes.

Vocabulary practice: *head, neck, shoulders, fingers, toes*

4

 45

👁 Look. 🔍 Find. ⭕ Circle. 💬 Say.

4 Language practice: *She / He / It has (two) (heads / necks / shoulders / fingers / toes).*

🎧 35 **Listen again.** ✏️ **Color.** 💬 **Say.**

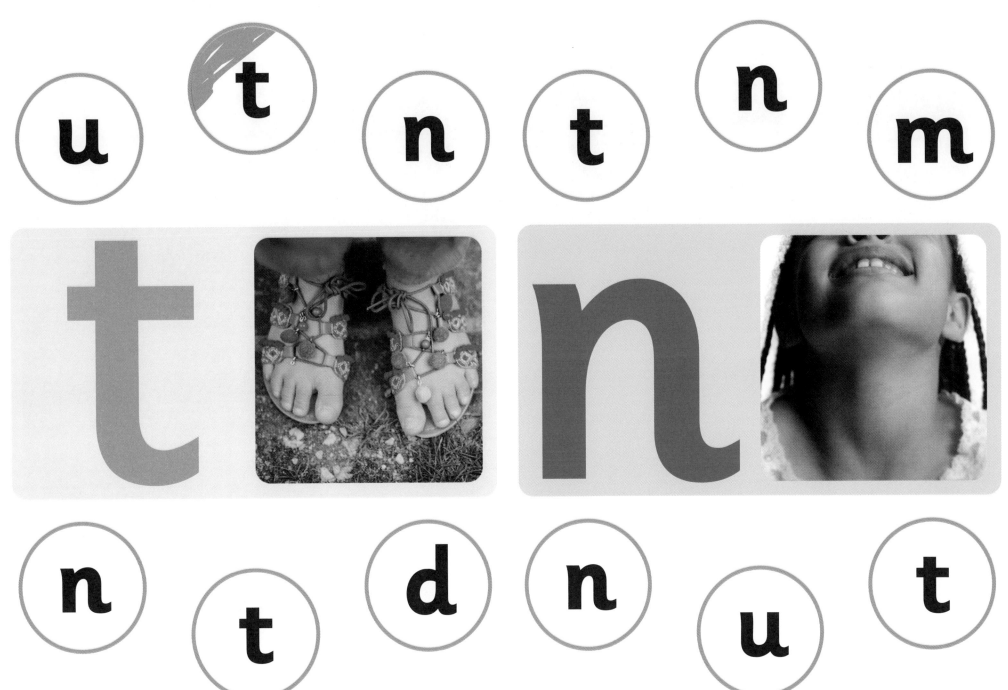

u t n t n m

t n

n t d n u t

👁 Look. 👆 Point. ⭕ Circle.

4 Literacy practice: Milo's shadow

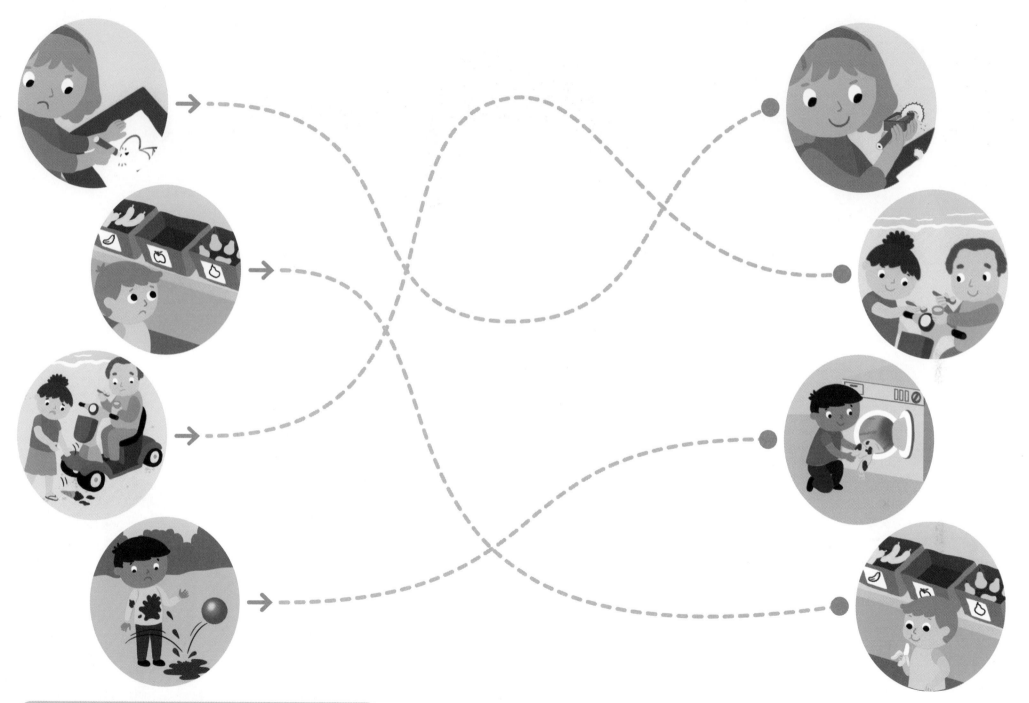

Look. Trace.

Look. Match. Say.

4 Vocabulary practice: *long, blond, straight, short, curly*

Look. Find. Circle. Say.

👁 Look. ✏ Draw. 💬 Say.

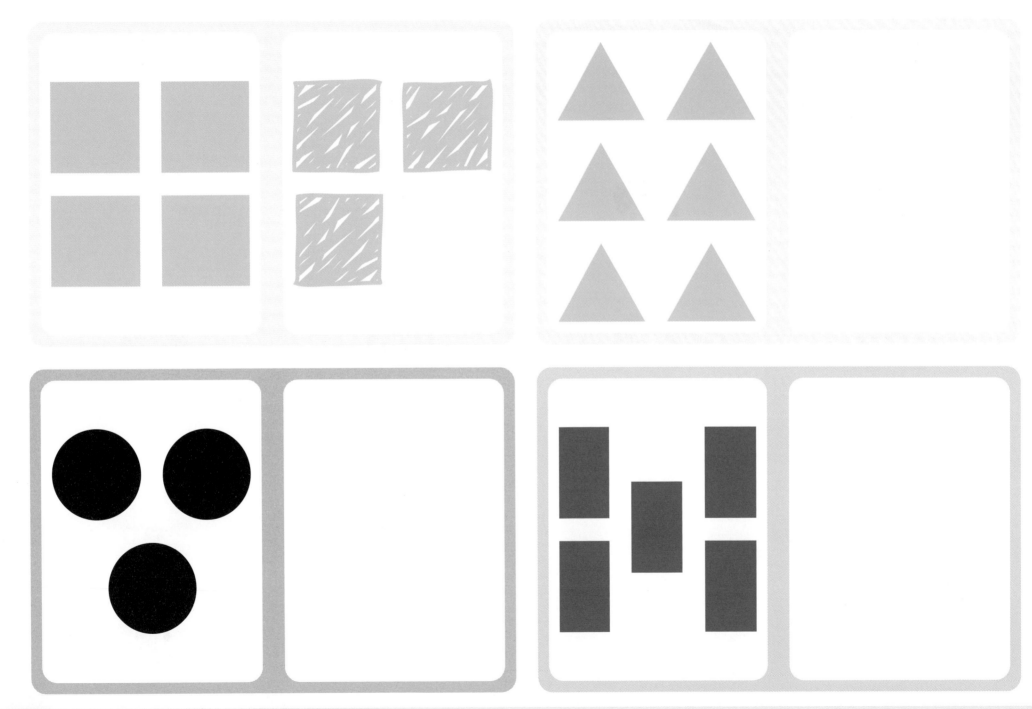

 Look. Match. Say.

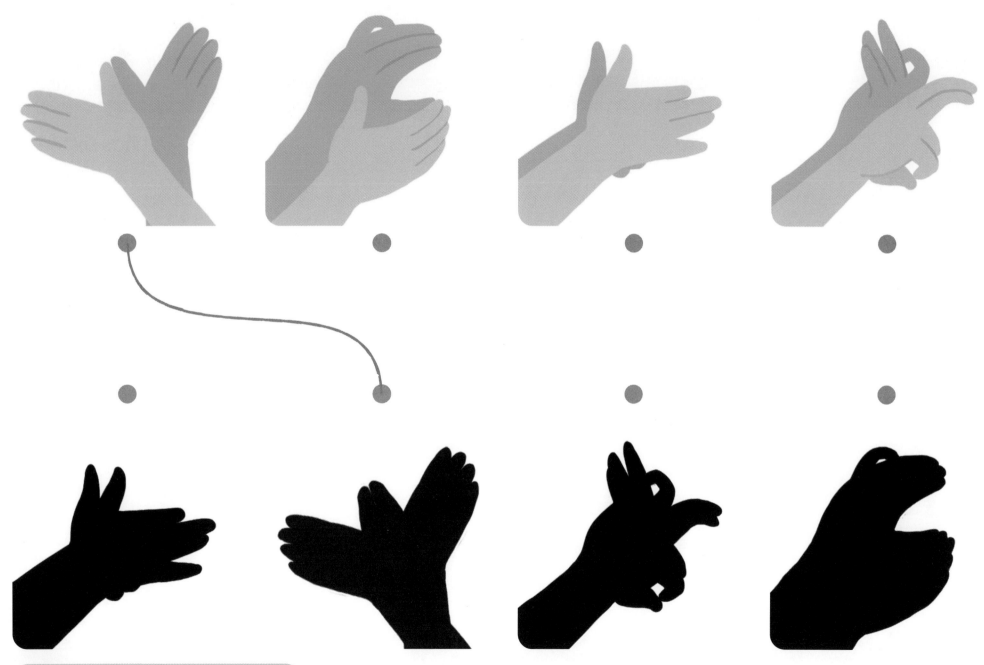

Look. **Draw.** **Say.**

It has six toes.

4 *It has (big / small) (fingers). It has (six) (toes). It has / It doesn't have (curly) hair.*

👆 **Point.** 💬 **Say.** ✏️ **Color.**

He has short curly hair.

Good job!

5 Outdoors

39 Listen again. 👁 Look. 🔘 Stick. 👆 Point.

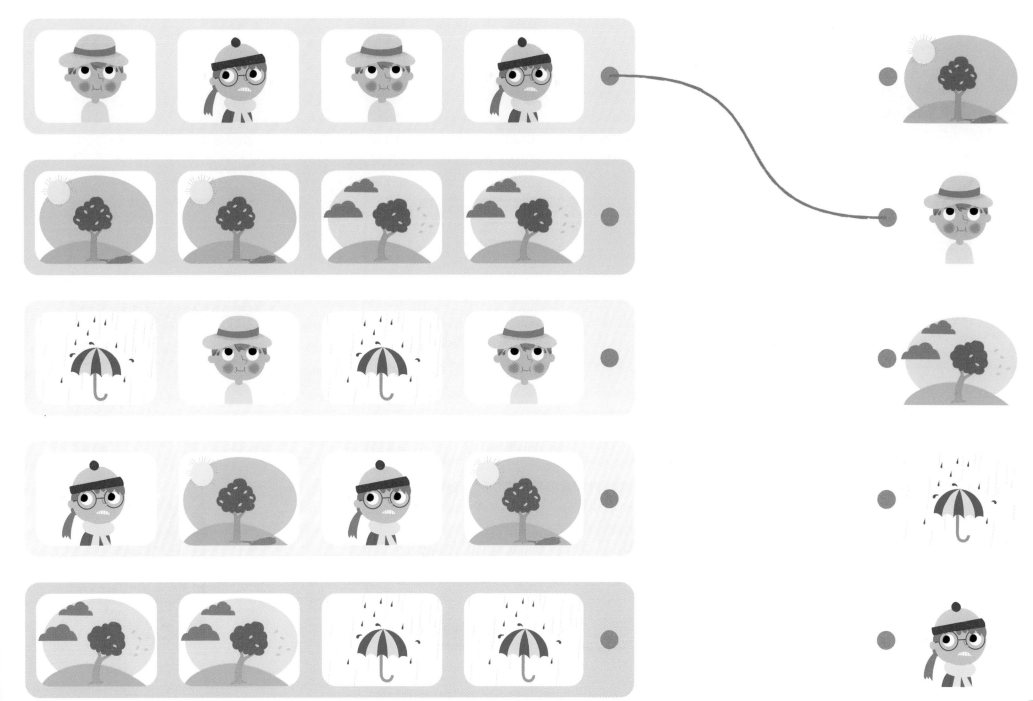 Look. 📖 Match. 💬 Say.

👁 Look. 🔍 Find. ✏ Color. 💬 Say.

At home 🏠

What's the weather like? Say.

5 **Language practice:** *What's the weather like? It's (hot / rainy / windy / cold / sunny).*

42 **Listen again.** 🖊 **Color.** 💬 **Say.**

s   e   s   h   n   s

s   h

h   b   s   h   u   h

👁 **Look.** 🔍 **Find.** ✏️ **Draw.**

🏠 **At home**

How do you celebrate nature?

⊙ Look. 🔍 Find. ◯ Circle. 💬 Say.

5 *Vocabulary practice: sunglasses, raincoat, boots, sweater, sandals*

👁 Look. 🔍 Find. ◯ Circle. 💬 Say.

🏠 **At home** Put on a sweater, boots, sunglasses, or a raincoat. Say.

Language practice: *I'm wearing (a raincoat / boots / sunglasses / sandals / a sweater).* ⑤ 63

👁 **Look.** ✋ **Count.** ◯ **Circle.** 💬 **Say.**

👁 **Look.** 🔍 **Find.** ⭕ **Circle.**

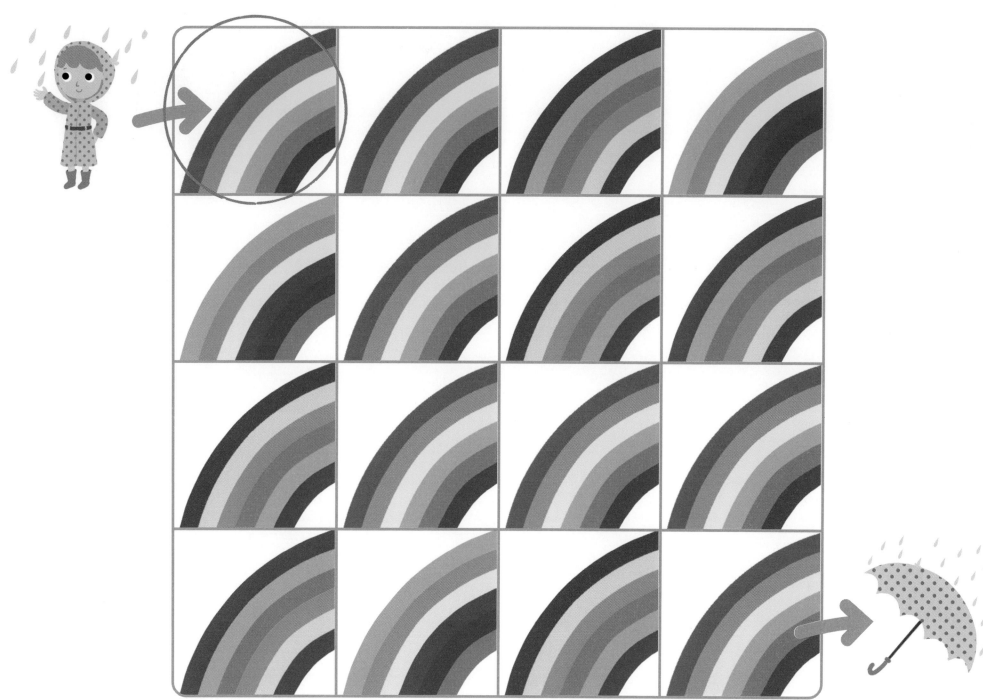

👁 Look. ✏ Draw. 💬 Say.

I'm wearing boots and a raincoat.

5 *I'm wearing (boots) and (a raincoat).*

👆 Point. 💬 Say. ✏️ Color.

It's windy.

Good job!

What's the weather like? It's (windy / sunny / rainy / hot / cold). 5

6 Animals

Listen again. **Look.** **Stick.** **Point.**

6 Unit topic introduction: Song practice

Look. Match. Say.

👁 Look. 🔍 Find. ⭕ Circle. 💬 Say.

6 **Language practice:** *It's a (cow / sheep / horse / chicken / goat). It has (four legs / a black face / small ears).*

🏠 **At home** Find a toy animal. Say.

50 🎧 **Listen again.** ✏️ **Color.** 💬 **Say.**

s

g

c

c

t

g

c

g

k

g

g

b

c

c

◉ Look. ☝ Point. ○ Circle.

Look. Trace.

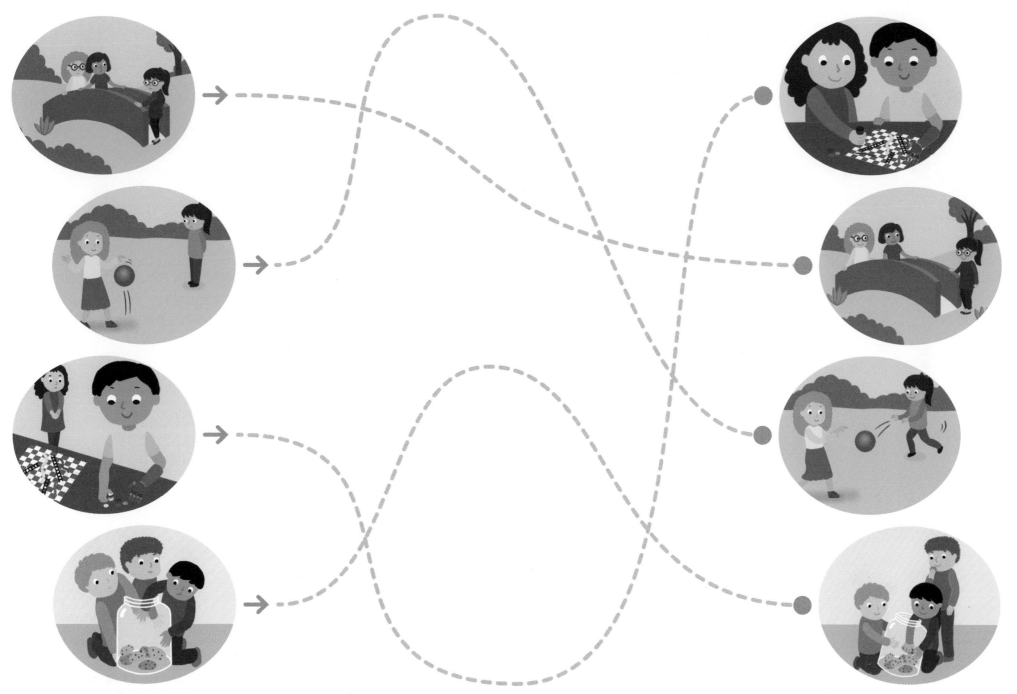

Look. Match. Say.

6 Vocabulary practice: *fly, jump, walk, swim, run*

Look. Find. Circle. Say.

👁 Look. 🔍 Find. ⭕ Circle. 💬 Say.

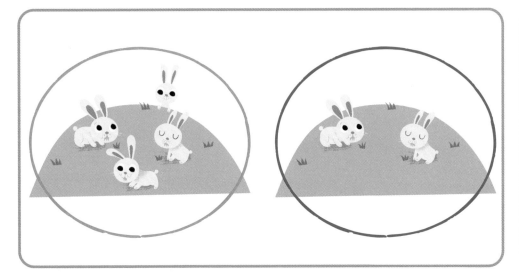

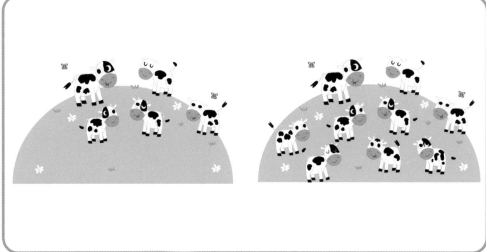

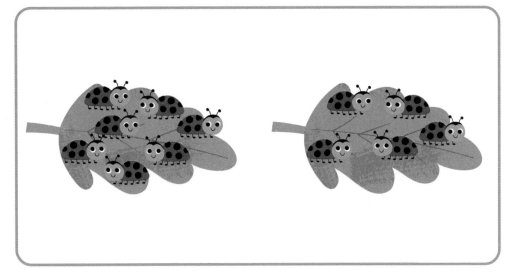

◉ Look. 🔍 Find. ◯ Circle.

🏠 **At home**

How do animals help you?

👁 **Look.** ✏️ **Draw.** 💬 **Say.**

It's a sheep.
It has four legs.

6 *It's a (sheep). It has (four legs / a gray face / small ears).*

👆 **Point.** 💬 **Say.** ✏️ **Color.**

A goat can jump.
A goat can't fly.

Good job!

👁 Look. 🔍 Find. 📖 Match. 💬 Say.

10

15

12

16

7 My favorite food

Look. Match. Say.

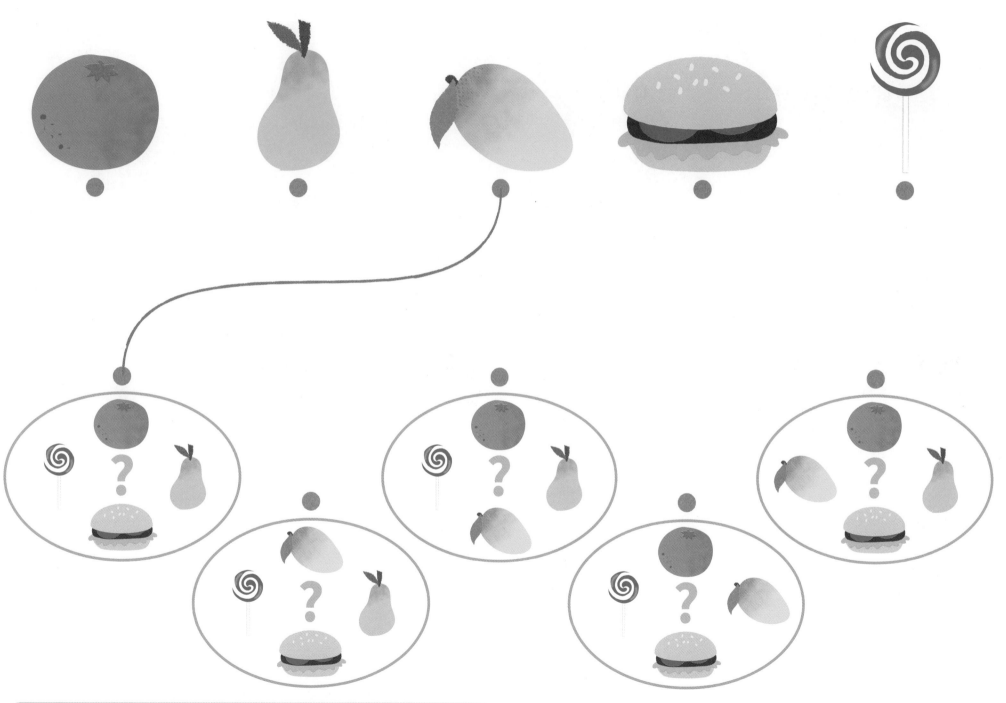

At home   Look in a store. Find an orange, a pear, a mango, a hamburger, or a lollipop.

Vocabulary practice: *orange, pear, mango, hamburger, lollipop*   7   83

Look. 🔍 **Find.** ◯ **Circle.** 💬 **Say.**

7 Language practice: *Can I have (an orange / a lollipop / a hamburger / a mango / a pear), please?*

🎧 59 **Listen again.** ✏️ **Color.** 💬 **Say.**

👁 **Look.** 🔍 **Find.** ✏️ **Draw.**

At home

How are you helpful at home?

Look. Find. Circle. Say.

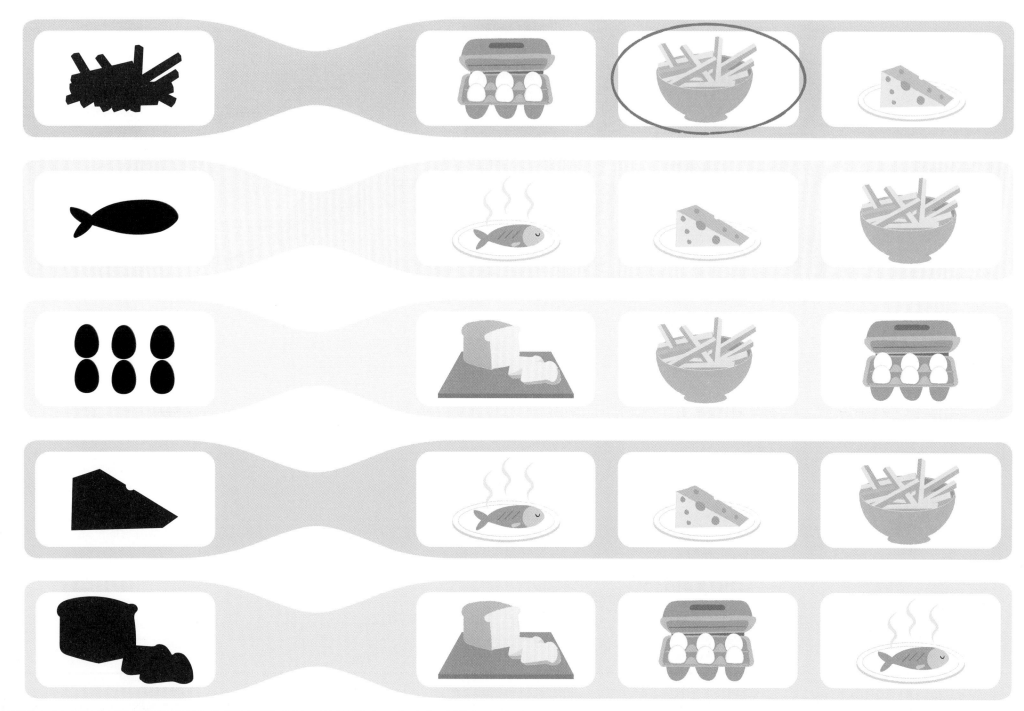

7 Vocabulary practice: *fries, fish, eggs, cheese, bread*

Look. ◯ Trace. 💬 Say.

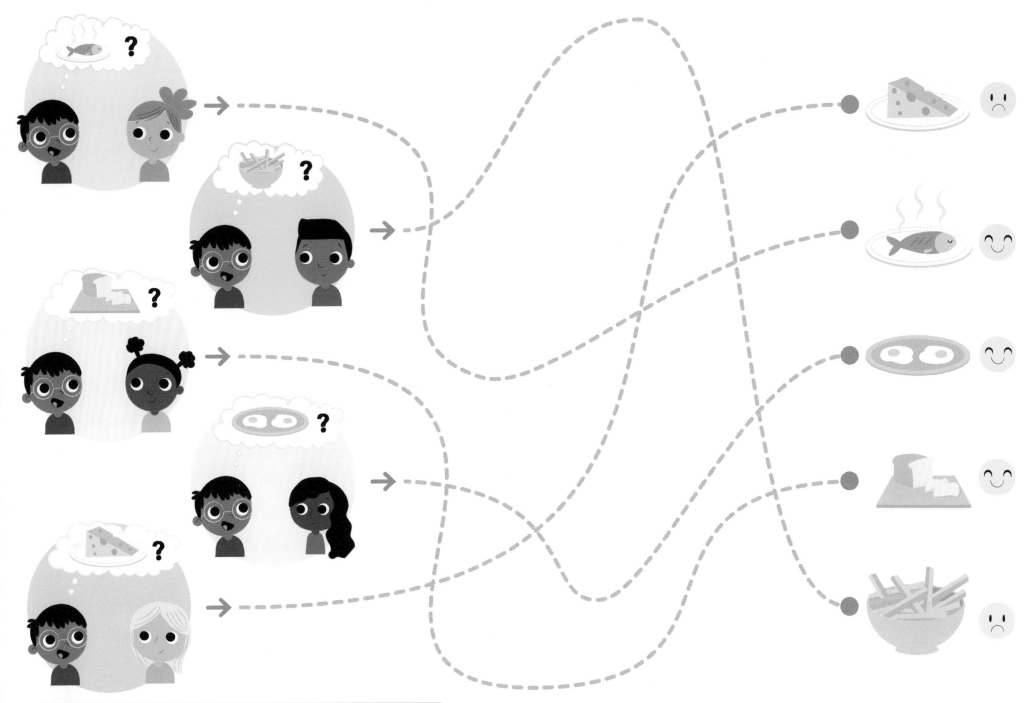

At home Talk to your family. Ask *Do you like eggs? Do you like fries?*

Language practice: *Do you like (fish / fries / bread / eggs / cheese)? Yes, I do. / No, I don't.*   7   89

👁 **Look.** ✋ **Count.** ⭕ **Circle.** 💬 **Say.**

17　(18)

17　18

17　18

17　18

⊙ **Look.** ○ **Circle.** ▬ **Say.**

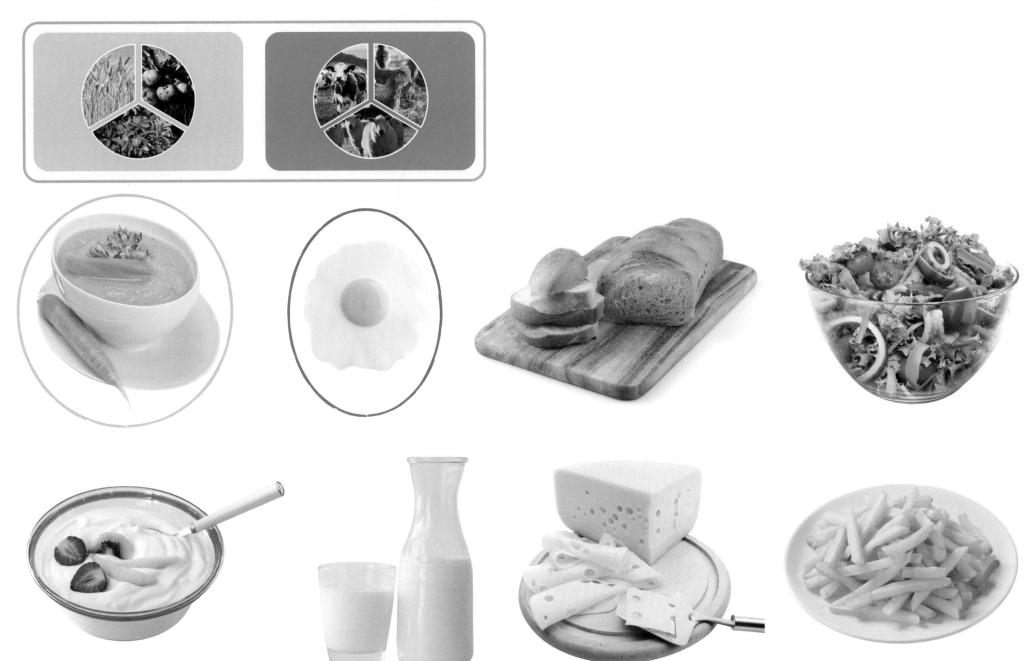

👁 **Look.** ✏ **Draw.** 💬 **Say.**

Do you like eggs?   Yes, I do.

7 *Do you like (cheese)? Yes, I do. / No, I don't.*

👆 **Point.** 💬 **Say.** ✏️ **Color.**

Can I have an orange, please?

Good job!

8 My senses

 Look. Find. Circle. Say.

At home

Ask *Can you taste an apple?*
Can you hear a bird?

8 **Language practice:** *Can you (hear / feel / smell / taste / see) (the bird)? Yes, I can. / No, I can't.*

🎧 **68** **Listen again.** ✏️ **Color.** 💬 **Say.**

j i z s j z

j z p j z j

g

👁 Look. 🔍 Find. ✏️ Color.

🏠 At home

Look around you. What things make you happy?

👁 Look. 🃏 Match. 💬 Say.

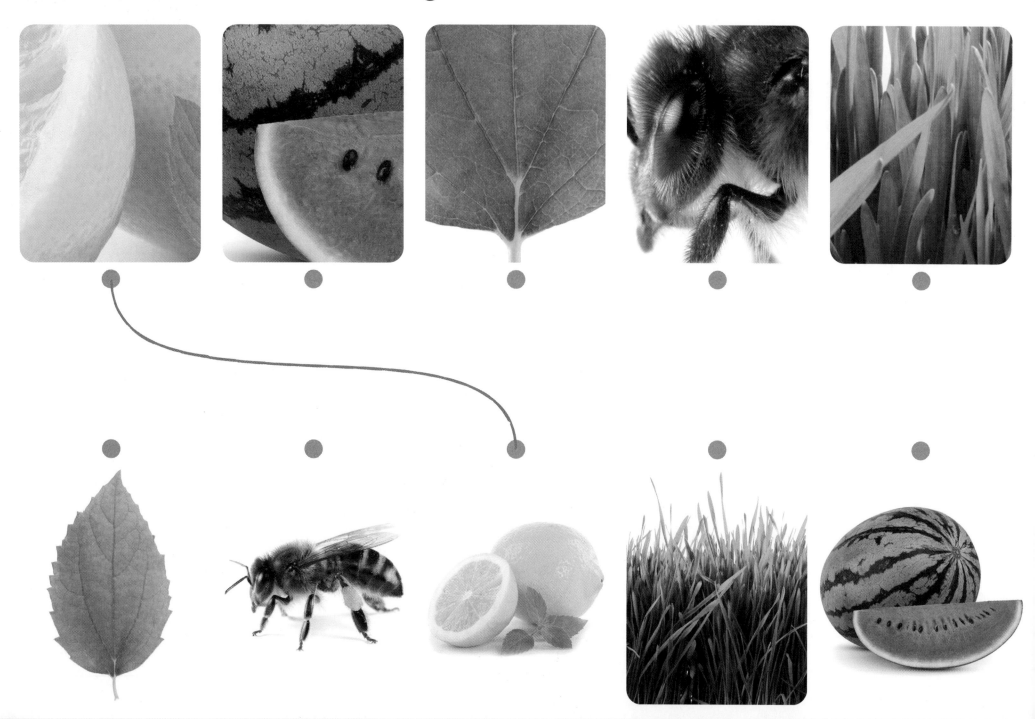

8 Vocabulary practice: *lemon, watermelon, leaf, bee, grass*

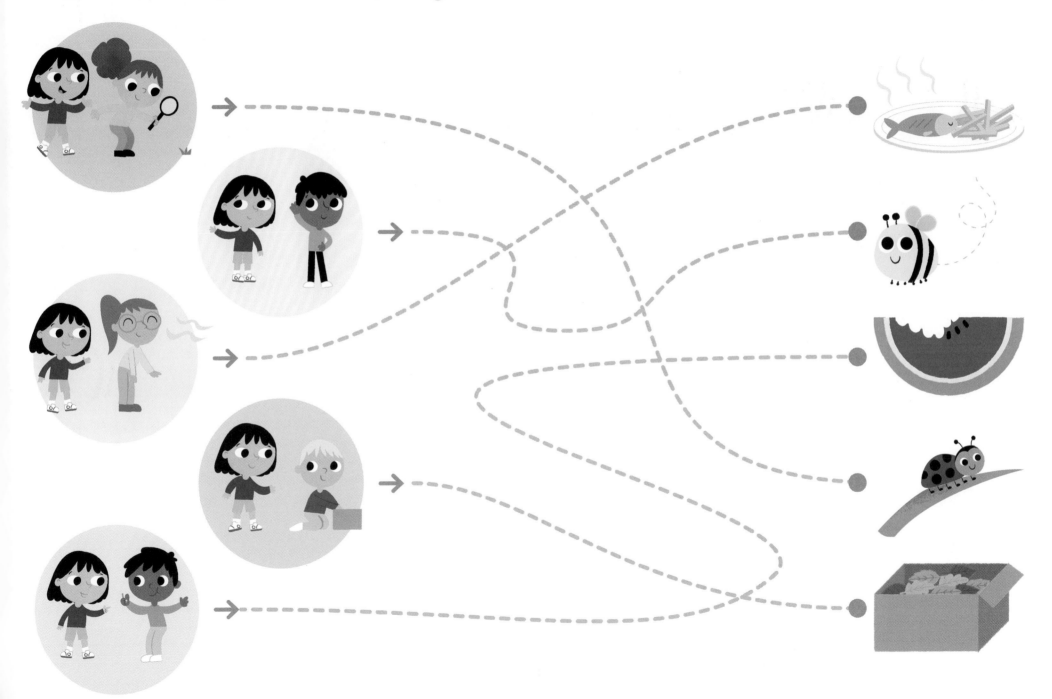 Look. ◯ Trace. 💬 Say.

At home Go outside. What can you smell? What can you hear?

Language practice: *What can you (see / hear / smell / feel / taste)? I can (see) a (ladybug).*

8

101

👁 Look. 📖 Match. 💬 Say.

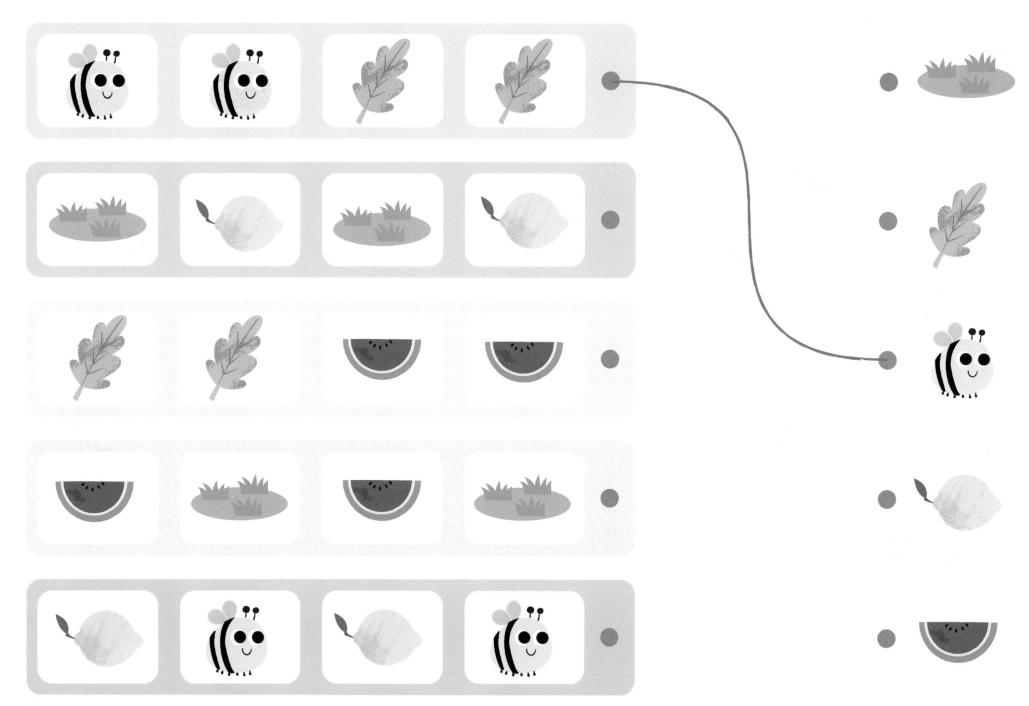

⊙ Look. ○ Circle. 🗩 Say.

👁 **Look.** ✏ **Draw.** 💬 **Say.**

I can hear a bird.

8 *What can you (feel / hear / see / smell / taste)? I can (hear) a (bird).*

 Point. 💬 **Say.** ✏️ **Color.**

Can you hear a frog?

Good job!

9 Vacations!

🎧 72 Listen again. 👁 Look. 💬 Stick. 👆 Point.

👁 Look. 📖 Match. 💬 Say.

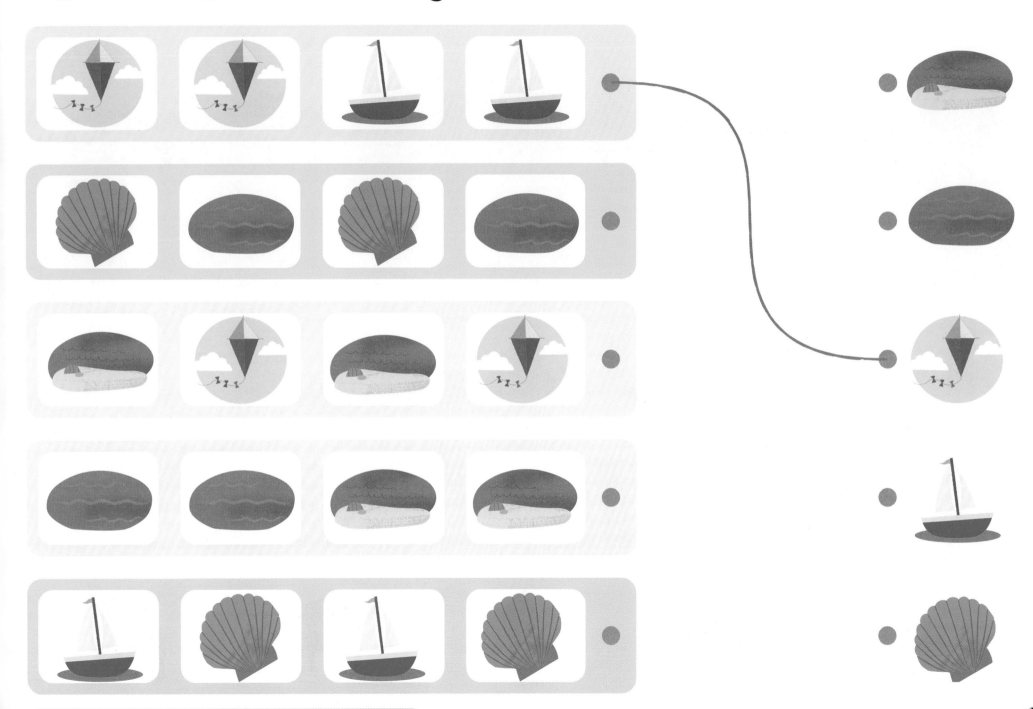

Find a picture of the beach.
What can you see?

👁 Look. 🔍 Find. ✋ Count. 💬 Say.

9 Language practice: *How many (boats) can you see? I can see (four) (boats).*

🎧 75 **Listen again.** ✏️ **Color.** 💬 **Say.**

👁 Look. ⭕ Trace.

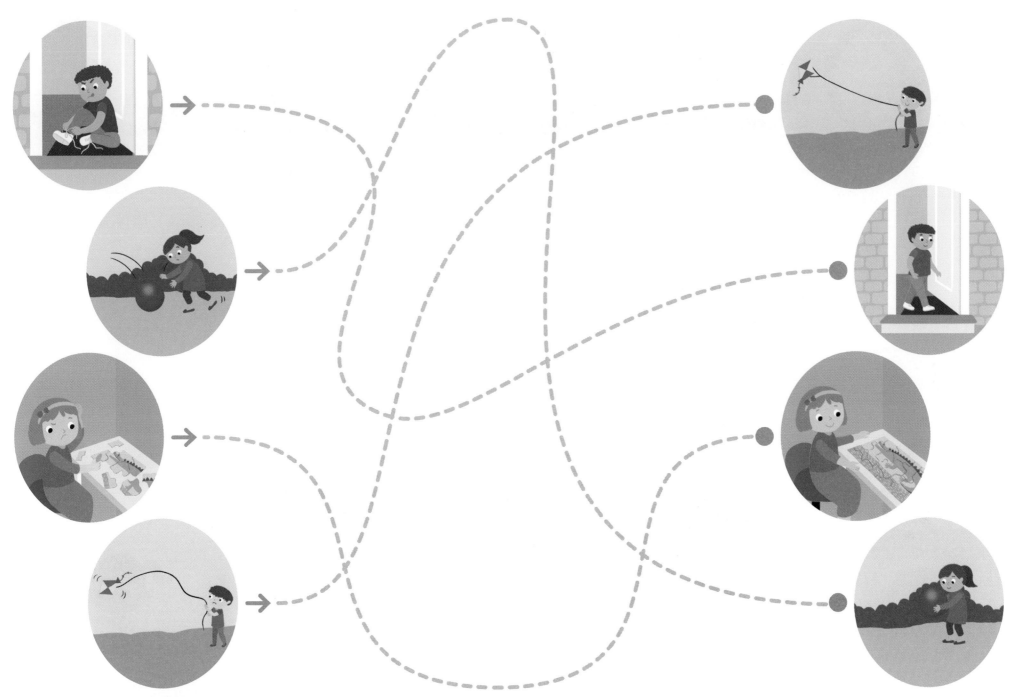

⊙ Look. 📖 Match. 💬 Say.

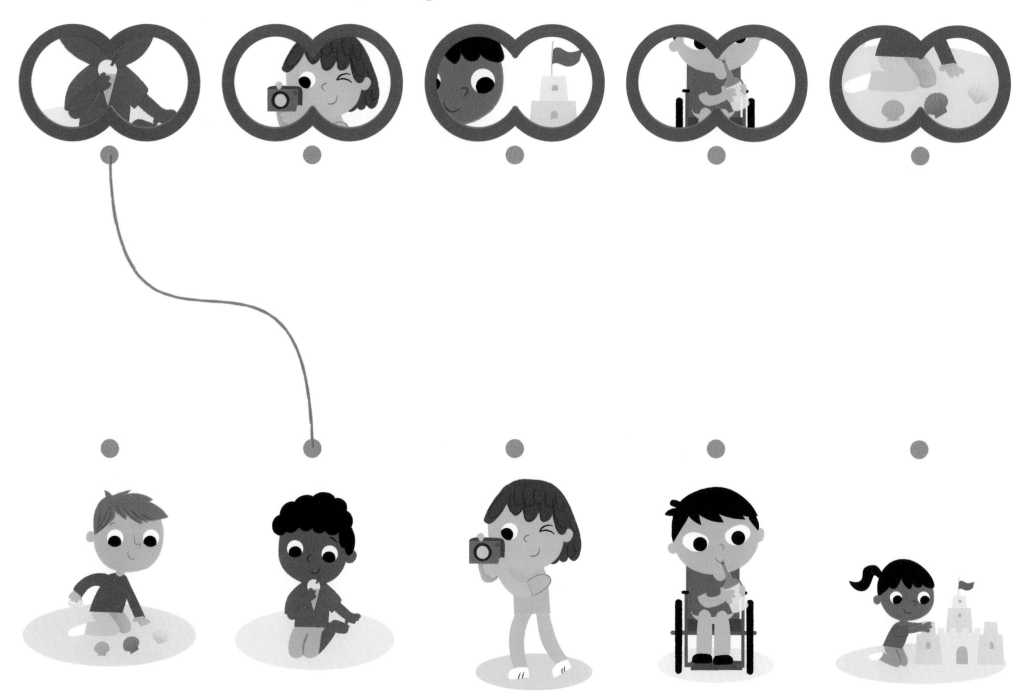

9 **Vocabulary practice:** *eating ice cream, taking pictures, making sandcastles, drinking lemonade, playing with shells*

Look. Find. Circle. Say.

👁 **Look.** ✋ **Count.** ⭕ **Circle.** 💬 **Say.**

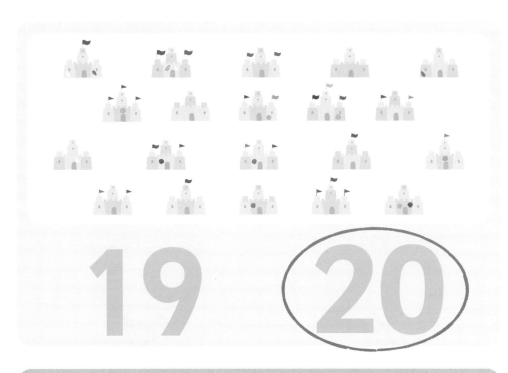

19 **⟨20⟩**

19 20

19   20

19   20

👁 Look. ✏ Color. 💬 Say.

👁 **Look.** ✏ **Draw.** 💬 **Say.**

I'm eating ice cream.

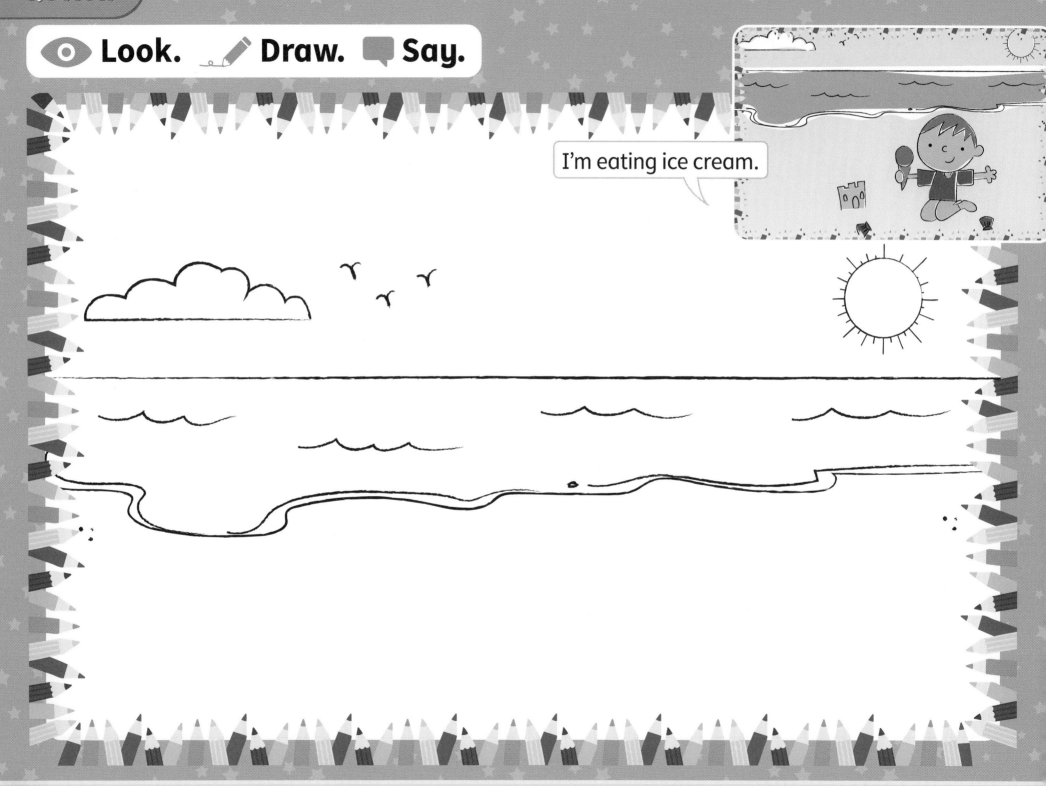

9 *I'm (eating ice cream) and (making sandcastles).*

👆 **Point.** 💬 **Say.** ✏️ **Color.**

I can see five boats.

Good job!

How many (boats / shells / sandcastles / kites / beaches) can you see? I can see (five) (boats). 9

Look. **Find.** **Match.** **Say.**

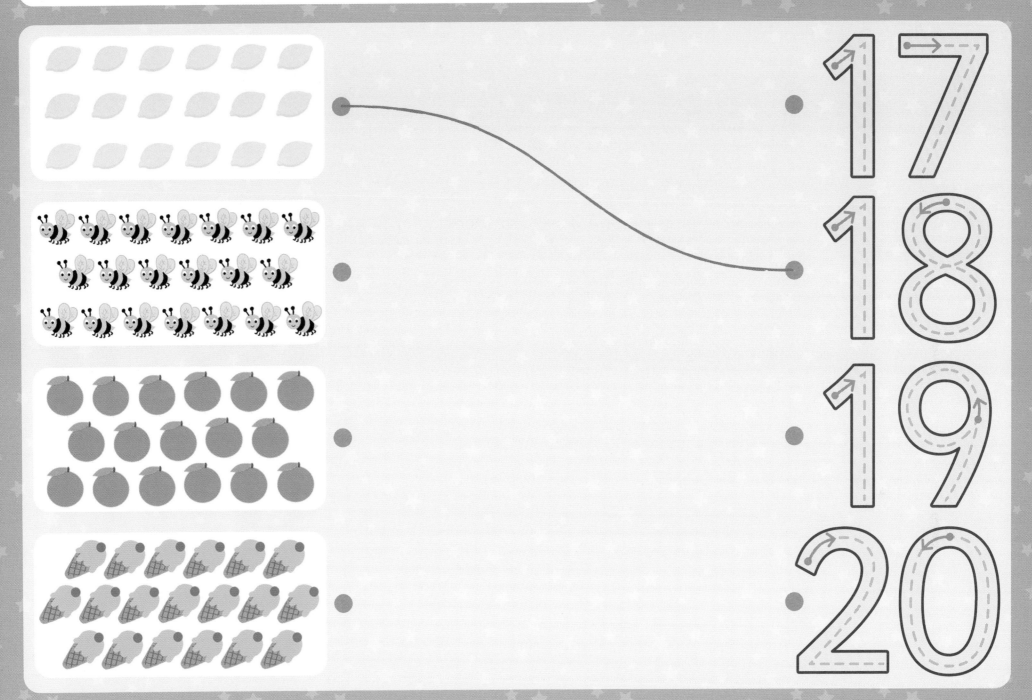

Thanks and Acknowledgements

The publishers and authors would like to thank the following contributors:
Book design and page make-up by Blooberry Design.
Cover design by Blooberry Design.
Freelance editing by Karen Cleveland Marwick and Stephanie Howard.
Editorial project management by Emma Ramírez.
Audio recording and production by Leon Chambers.
Original songs and chants by Robert Lee.
Songs and chants production by Jake Carter.

The authors and publishers acknowledge the following sources of copyright material and are grateful for the permissions granted. While every effort has been made, it has not always been possible to identify the sources of all the material used, or to trace all copyright holders. If any omissions are brought to our notice, we will be happy to include the appropriate acknowledgements on reprinting and in the next update to the digital edition, as applicable.

Key: U = Unit.

Photography

All photos are sourced from Getty Images.
U1: Christopher Hopefitch/The Image Bank; cristinairanzo/Moment Open; Mai Vu/iStock/Getty Images Plus; **U2:** real444/E+; Robert Kneschke/EyeEm; Xuanyu Han/Moment; GlobalStock/iStock/Getty Images Plus; XiXinXing; Daniela Jovanovska-Hristovska/E+; Hill Street Studios/DigitalVision; XiXinXing/iStock/Getty Images Plus; Tara Moore/DigitalVision; monkeybusinessimages/iStock/Getty Images Plus; Julialine/iStock/Getty Images Plus; Markus Bernhard/Stone; Kemal Can Habip/EyeEm; Image Source; Jetta Productions Inc./DigitalVision; mmg1design/iStock/Getty Images Plus; Kevin Dodge; adamkaz/E+; John Burke/Photolibrary/Getty Images Plus; Mai Vu/iStock/Getty Images Plus; **U3:** Melissa Ross/Moment; Martin Deja/Moment; Adam Hester/Photodisc; Camille Tokerud/Stone; Mai Vu/iStock/Getty Images Plus; **U4:** AnnaNahabed/iStock/Getty Images Plus; Rubberball; Pankaj & Insy Shah; PhotoAlto/Sandro Di Carlo Darsa/PhotoAlto Agency RF Collections; Mai Vu/iStock/Getty Images Plus; **U5:** Sally Anscombe/DigitalVision; Peter Cade/Stone; Xuanyu Han/Moment; SbytovaMN/iStock/Getty Images Plus; ArtistGNDphotography/E+; bgfoto/E+; twomeows/Moment; Jon Feingersh Photography Inc/DigitalVision; Mai Vu/iStock/Getty Images Plus; **U6:** Westend61; Danita Delimont/Gallo Images/Getty Images Plus; Australian Scenics/Photolibrary/Getty Images Plus; monkeybusinessimages/iStock/Getty Images Plus; Don Farrall/Photodisc; Martin Ruegner/Photographer's Choice RF; Zoe Esteban/EyeEm; Tuul & Bruno Morandi/The Image Bank; Anup Shah/Stone; Sharon Vos-Arnold/Moment Open; Cynthia Lempitsky/iStock/Getty Images Plus; Jose Luis Pelaez Inc/DigitalVision; Mai Vu/iStock/Getty Images Plus; **U7:** atoss/iStock/Getty Images Plus; duckycards/E+; gerenme/E+; martin-dm/E+; Randy Mayor/Photolibrary/Getty Images Plus; franckreporter/E+; pixelprof/iStock/Getty Images Plus; Henry Arden/Cultura; Inacio Pires/EyeEm; Yuji Sakai/DigitalVision; VLIET/E+; Zoonar/D.Dzinnik; Kamal Iklil/Moment; R.Tsubin/Moment; ATU Images/The Image Bank; Maximilian Stock Ltd./Photolibrary/Getty Images Plus; krisanapong detraphiphat/Moment; Creativ Studio Heinemann; vikif/iStock/Getty Images Plus; Mai Vu/iStock/Getty Images Plus; **U8:** CliqueImages/Taxi/Getty Images Plus; Azure-Dragon/iStock/Getty Images Plus; FourOaks/iStock/Getty Images Plus; Paul Bradbury/OJO Images; Adam Smigielski/E+; Boonchuay1970/iStock/Getty Images Plus; Avalon_Studio/E+; arlindo71/E+; Creativ Studio Heinemann; Creativ Studio Heinemann; imagenavi; manolo guijarro/Moment; Vicki Jauron, Babylon and Beyond Photography/Moment; Adria Photography/Moment; bkindler/E+; Nick Dolding/Stone; HotDuckZ/iStock/Getty Images Plus; Jose Luis Pelaez Inc/DigitalVision; Johner Images; John Foxx/Stockbyte; Mai Vu/iStock/Getty Images Plus; **U9:** AlexLMX/iStock/Getty Images Plus; Boonchuay1970/iStock/Getty Images Plus; JackF/iStock/Getty Images Plus; Maciej Nicgorski/EyeEm; PM Images/Stone; Mai Vu/iStock/Getty Images Plus; Nazman Mizan/EyeEm.

Illustrations
Amy Zhing; Beatriz Castro; Begoña Corbalán; Isabelle Nicolle; Noopur Thakur; Louise Forshaw; and Collaborate artists.
Cover illustration by Collaborate Agency.

Good job!

Good job!

Good job!

 **4 My body** (Page 44)

 **5 Outdoors** (Page 56)

 **6 Animals** (Page 68)

Good job!

Good job!

Good job!

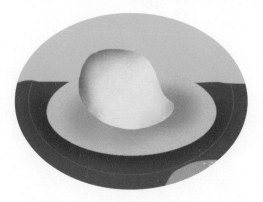

Good job!

Good job!

Good job!